PIANO

All Sorts

INITIAL–GRADE 1

Edited and selected by John York

Faber Music in association with Trinity College London

Bromley Libraries

3 0128 03072758 3

© 2002 by Faber Music Ltd and Trinity College London
First published in 2002 by Faber Music Ltd
in association with Trinity College London
Bloomsbury House 74–77 Great Russell Street London WC1B 3DA
Cover illustration by Vikki Liogier/Illustrationweb.com
Music processed by Jackie Leigh
Printed in England by Caligraving Ltd
All rights reserved

ISBN10: 0-571-52113-4
EAN13: 978-0-571-52113-5

Please note that the metronome marks given are for guidance only and are
generally kept slightly on the slow side. In a few instances I have made minor
simplifications to pieces to keep within the grading of the collection, but on no
occasion have I altered the character of the music.

John York

To buy Faber Music or Trinity publications or to find out about the full range of titles
available please contact your local music retailer or Faber Music sales enquiries:

Faber Music Ltd, Burnt Mill, Elizabeth Way, Harlow CM20 2HX
Tel: +44 (0)1279 82 89 82   Fax: +44 (0)1279 82 89 83
sales@fabermusic.com   fabermusic.com

Contents

THE COOL WIZARD!

Pam Wedgwood

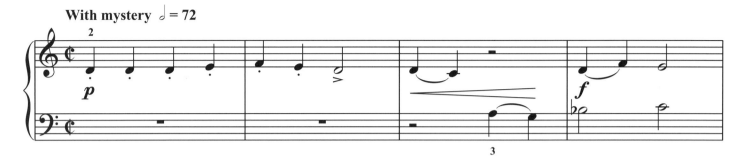

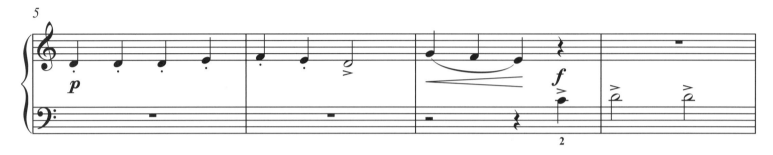

PODGY TOURERS

Gary Carpenter

4   © 2002 by Faber Music Ltd and Trinity College London

MINUET

Jean-Baptiste Lully
(1632–1687)

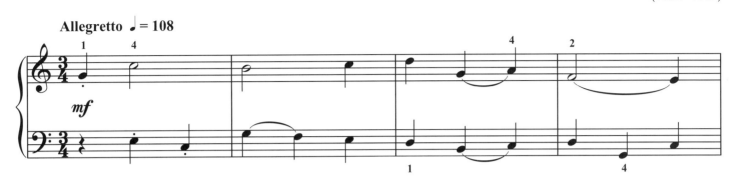

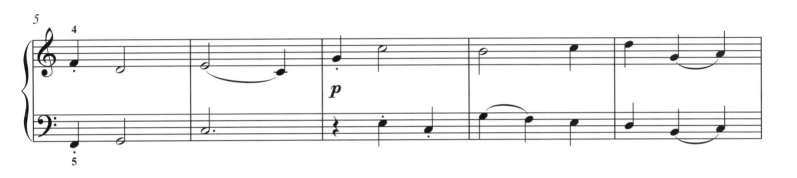

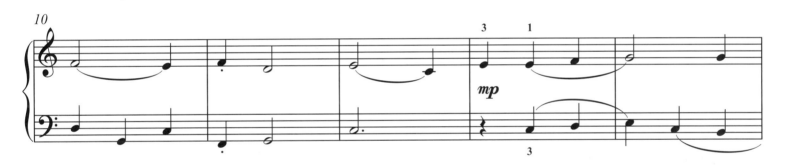

5

ALMOST A CANON

FAST EIN KANON

Johann Joseph Fux
(1660–1741)

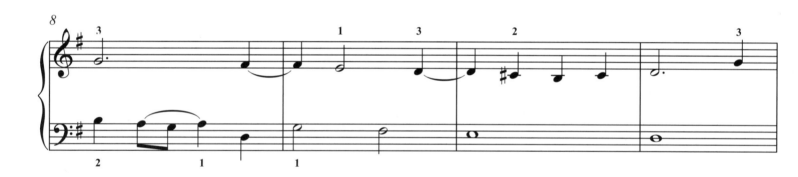

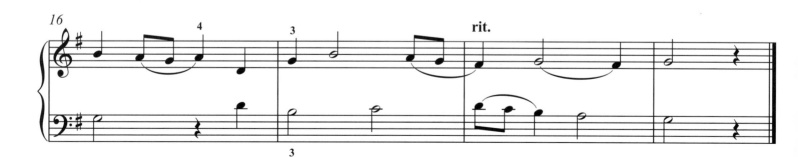

EENIE, MEENIE, MINIE, MO

Either decide the order of fragments on the spot (i.e., play a fragment
and *then* decide what comes next), or decide the order beforehand.
Various types of patterns are possible: **a**b**a**c**a**d**a** …, **abcadcaec** …, etc.
Dynamics are left to the discretion of the student.

Snorri Sigfús Birgisson

a

b

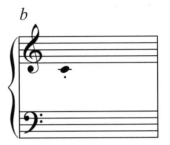

c

d

e

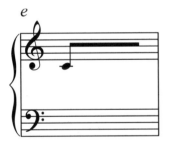

(Start wherever you like
and go wherever you like,
from wherever you are …)

f

g

© Copyright Snorri Sigfús Birgisson 1987

A LITTLE TUNE

Dmitri Kabalevsky
(1904–1987)

© Copyright 1967 by Anglo Soviet Music Press Ltd, a Boosey & Hawkes Company, for the UK,
British Commonwealth (excluding Canada) and Eire. Reproduced by permission of
Boosey & Hawkes Music Publishers Ltd for all territories of the world.

MARCHING

Dmitri Kabalevsky
(1904–1987)

© Copyright 1967 by Anglo Soviet Music Press Ltd, a Boosey & Hawkes Company, for the UK,
British Commonwealth (excluding Canada) and Eire. Reproduced by permission of
Boosey & Hawkes Music Publishers Ltd for all territories of the world.

A SAD TALE

Dmitri Kabalevsky
(1904–1987)

© Copyright 1967 by Anglo Soviet Music Press Ltd, a Boosey & Hawkes Company, for the UK,
British Commonwealth (excluding Canada) and Eire. Reproduced by permission of
Boosey & Hawkes Music Publishers Ltd for all territories of the world.

TAKING IT EASY

John York

MAZURKA

E Szönyi

 © 1969 by Editio Musica Budapest

MINUET

Franz Joseph Haydn
(1732–1809)

HOPPITY-HOP

P Járdányi
(1920–1966)

12   © 1969 by Editio Musica Budapest

MENUET EN RONDEAU

Jean-Philippe Rameau
(1683–1764)

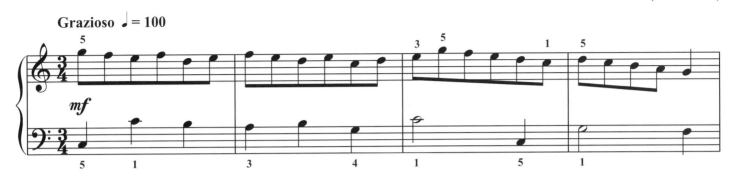

RIGAUDON

Con brio, tempo giusto ♩ = 126

Georg Philipp Telemann
(1681–1767)

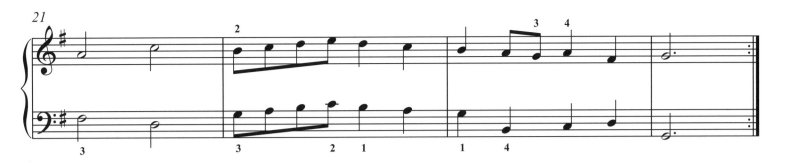

LITTLE SONG

Philip Martin

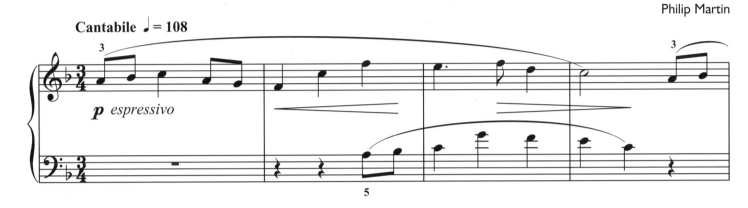

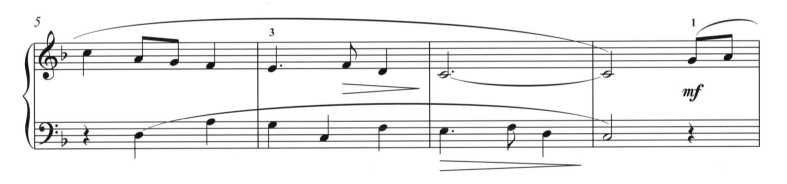

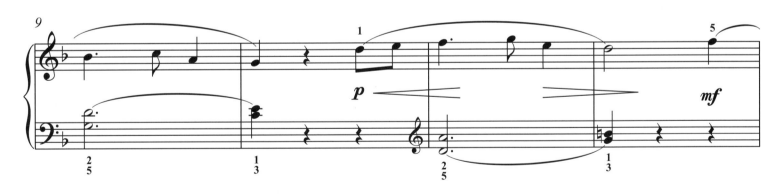

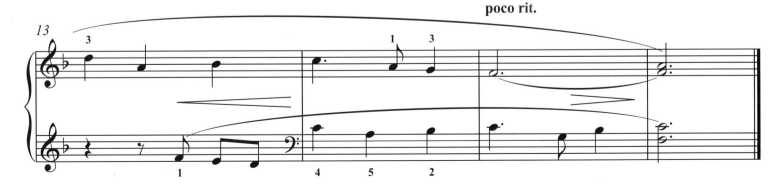

© 2002 The Contemporary Music Centre, Ireland. Taken from *Pick-up Pieces* by Philip Martin, published by the Contemporary Music Centre, Ireland, available from www.cmc.ie.

STUDY

Ferdinand Beyer
(1803–1863)

KLAVIERSTÜCK

Wolfgang Amadeus Mozart
(1756–1791)

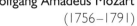

THE KEYS OF CANTERBURY

arranged by **John Kember**

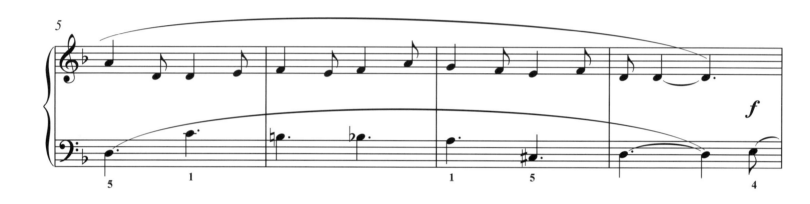

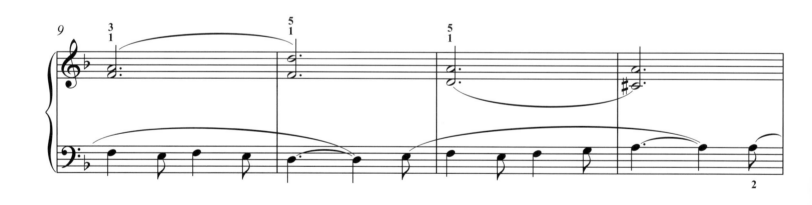

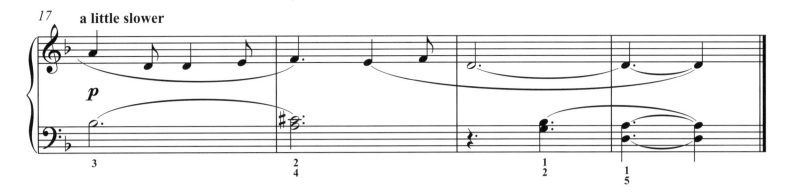

GERMAN DANCE

Ludwig van Beethoven
(1770–1827)

IMPERTINENCE

George Frideric Handel
(1685–1759)

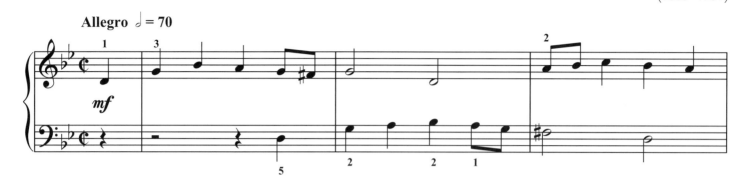

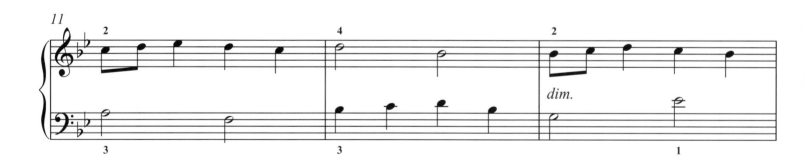

MENUETTO

Wolfgang Amadeus Mozart
(1756–1791)

GIGUE

Leopold Mozart
(1719–1787)

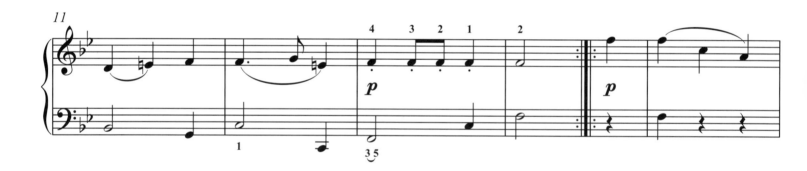

HANDS TOGETHER

Andrew Toovey

TO BEGIN WITH

Nicolai von Wilm
(1834–1911)

Mässig (Moderato) ♩ = 108

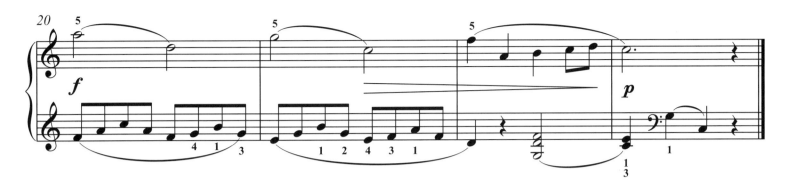

BADINAGE

Arcangelo Corelli
(1653–1713)

ENCHANTING

Christopher Norton

* The lower note may be played then released in the case of a small hand.

© Copyright 2002 by Boosey & Hawkes Music Publishers Ltd.
Reproduced by permission of Boosey & Hawkes Music Publishers Ltd.

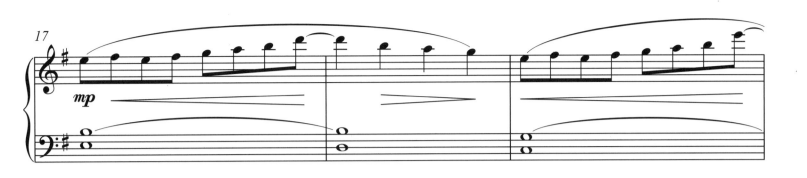

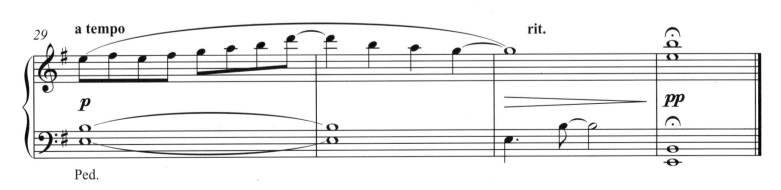

ANDANTE

Thomas Attwood
(1765–1838)

DANZA

F Szabó
(1902–1969)

© 1969 by Editio Musica Budapest

ANDANTINO

Felix Le Couppey
(1811–1887)

Educational publications from Faber Music

PIANO

Up-Grade! Piano Grades 0–1 *Pam Wedgwood*
ISBN 0-571-51737-4

More Up-Grade! Piano Grades 0–1 *Pam Wedgwood*
ISBN 0-571-51956-3

Up-Grade! Piano Grades 1–2 *Pam Wedgwood*
ISBN 0-571-51560-6

Up-Grade! Piano Grades 2–3 *Pam Wedgwood*
ISBN 0-571-51561-4

Up-Grade! Piano Grades 3–4 *Pam Wedgwood*
ISBN 0-571-51775-7

Jazz piano plus one *John Kember*
ISBN 0-571-52373-0

Jazz piano studies 1 *John Kember*
ISBN 0-571-52400-1

Jazz piano studies 2 *John Kember*
ISBN 0-571-52450-8

Very Easy Little Peppers *Elissa Milne*
ISBN 0-571-52312-9

Easy Little Peppers *Elissa Milne*
ISBN 0-571-52313-7

FABER ƒƒ MUSIC

To buy Faber Music publications or to find out about the full range of titles available
please contact your local music retailer or Faber Music sales enquiries:

Faber Music Ltd, Burnt Mill, Elizabeth Way, Harlow CM20 2HX
Tel: +44 (0) 1279 82 89 82   Fax: +44 (0) 1279 82 89 83
sales@fabermusic.com   fabermusic.com   expressprintmusic.com

Up-Grade!

Light relief between grades

Pamela Wedgwood

Tired of the same old exam pieces?
Looking for something to bridge the gap between grades?
Need a bit of light relief? *Up-Grade!* is for you!

Pam Wedgwood's inimitable, original style is guaranteed to breathe new life into your playing—
the varied pieces and duets in these bright new collections range from toe-tapping jazzy
numbers to more classical styles, all designed to ease you gently on towards the next grade.

Up-Grade! Piano Grades 0–1	ISBN 0-571-51737-4
More Up-Grade! Piano Grades 0–1	ISBN 0-571-51956-3
Up-Grade! Piano Grades 1–2	ISBN 0-571-51560-6
More Up-Grade! Piano Grades 1–2	ISBN 0-571-52420-6
Up-Grade! Piano Grades 2–3	ISBN 0-571-51561-4
More Up-Grade! Piano Grades 2–3	ISBN 0-571-52421-4
Up-Grade! Piano Grades 3–4	ISBN 0-571-51775-7
Up-Grade! Piano Grades 4–5	ISBN 0-571-51776-5
Up-Grade Pop! Piano Grades 0–1	ISBN 0-571-52474-5
Up-Grade Pop! Piano Grades 1–2	ISBN 0-571-52475-3
Up-Grade Pop! Piano Grades 2–3	ISBN 0-571-53124-5
Up-Grade Pop! Piano Grades 3–4	ISBN 0-571-53125-3
Up-Grade Jazz! Piano Grades 0–1	ISBN 0-571-52476-1
Up-Grade Jazz! Piano Grades 1–2	ISBN 0-571-52477-X
Up-Grade Jazz! Piano Grades 2–3	ISBN 0-571-53122-9
Up-Grade Jazz! Piano Grades 3–4	ISBN 0-571-53123-7
Up-Grade Christmas! Piano Grades 0–1	ISBN 0-571-52953-4
Up-Grade Christmas! Piano Grades 1–2	ISBN 0-571-52954-2
Up-Grade! Piano Duets Grades 0–1	ISBN 0-571-53264-0

Lighten up and move on with Up-Grade!

FABER *ff* MUSIC

To buy Faber Music publications or to find out about the full range of titles available
please contact your local music retailer or Faber Music sales enquiries:

Faber Music Ltd, Burnt Mill, Elizabeth Way, Harlow CM20 2HX
Tel: +44 (0) 1279 82 89 82   Fax: +44 (0) 1279 82 89 83
sales@fabermusic.com   fabermusic.com   expressprintmusic.com